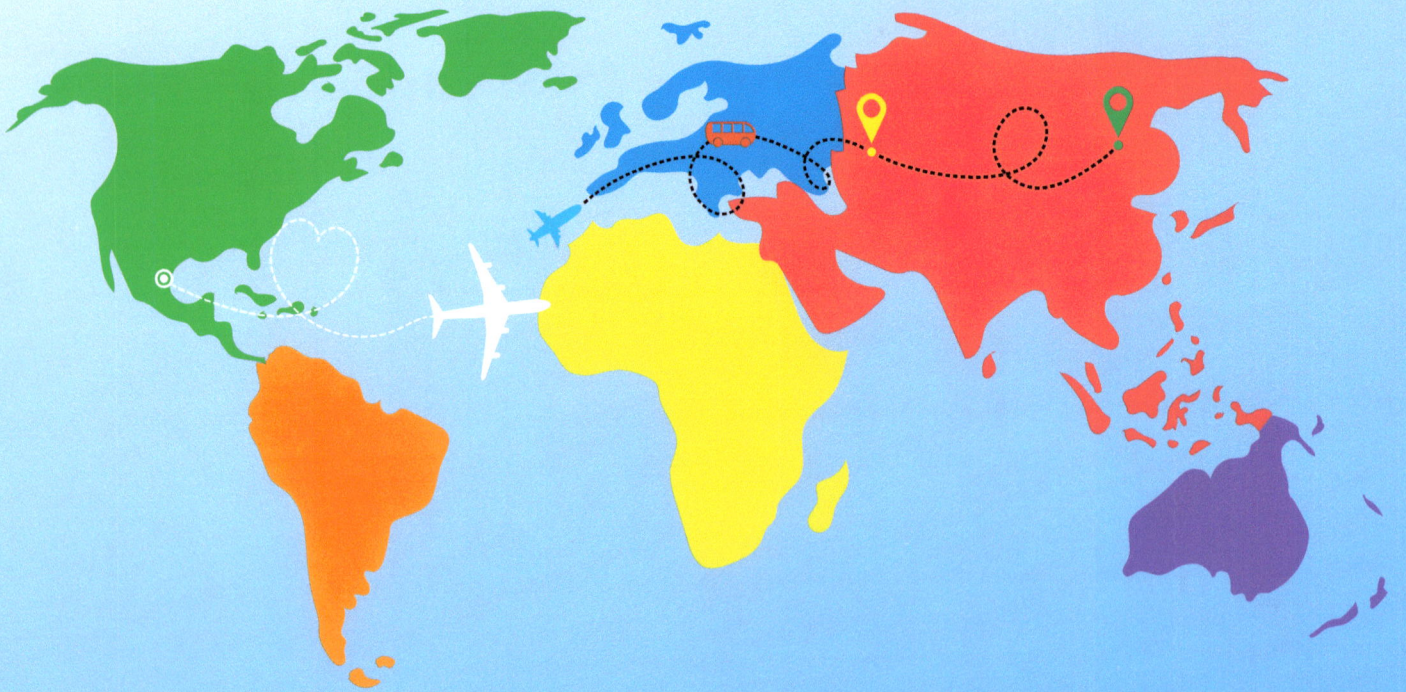

Follow your heart.
It knows the way.

Dedicated to my son Rocean.
Thank you for being my guiding star, my shining light. The inspiration behind everything I do. I love you!

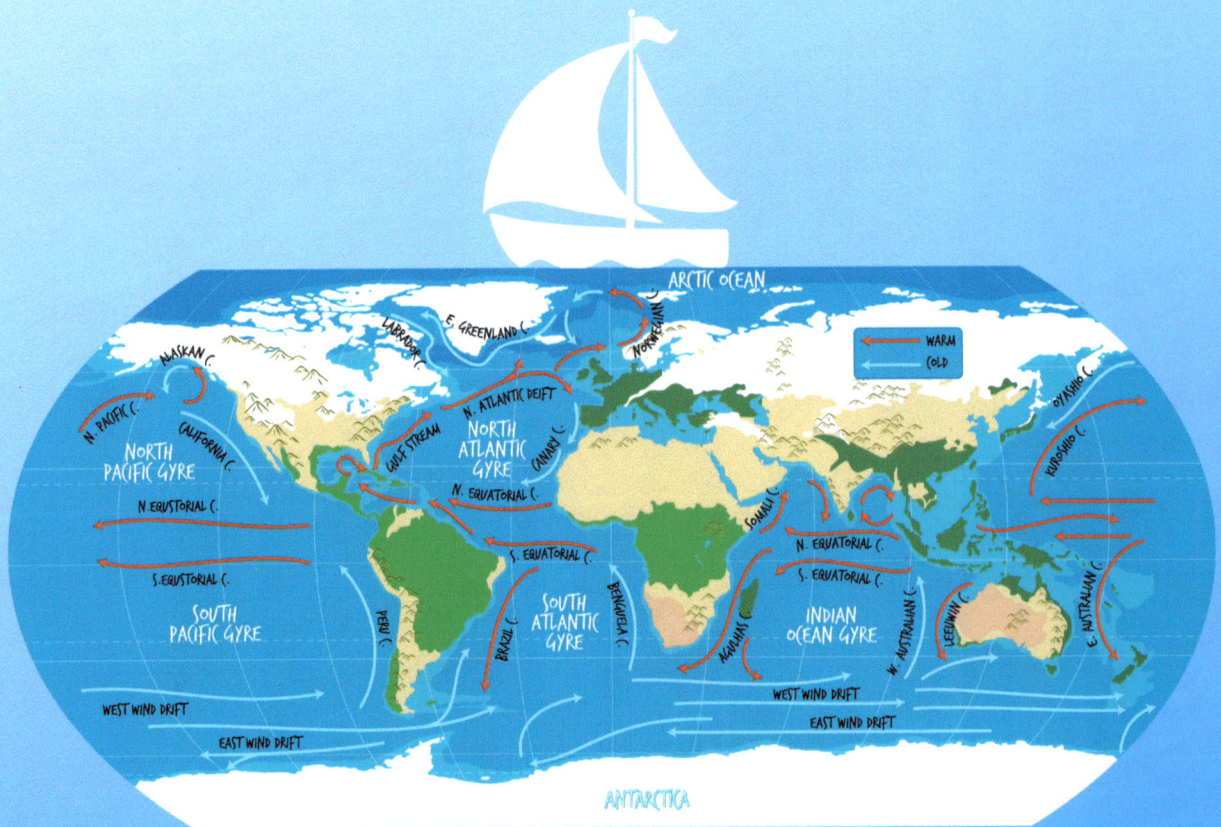

Keep exploring and loving this beautiful earth.

Dear Earth

The very first story!

By
Olivia Frank

One star filled evening. A curious little boy was thinking about the Earth. He had so many questions. He decided to write a letter! He told his friends about his letter after they were done playing that night. Turns out, the others had questions about Earth too! Then, they all began to write letters!

Earth was so happy to hear they were interested in learning more.

And so it begins...

One

letter

at

a

time

Earth began to answer with excitement!

Earth replies with a giggle,

Each day I spin slowly as I rotate around the sun. But to me its like dancing! As I spin, when I am facing the sun it is daytime. The other half of me that is not facing the sun, it's night time! Amazing right?!

Did you know it takes one year for Earth to make a full rotation around the sun. That's 365 days!

Dear Earth,

Why are there
so many different
animals?

With Love,
Vivienne, Max, & Sasha

I love bunnies!

Don't worry
Be hoppy!

Earth says.

Each animal is special.
Some help the planet.

Others work hard all day to survive. All creature's, just like humans, are different in their own way.

Different is good!

We are all here to do our part. Special in our own way. It's up to each of us to figure out what our special talent is!

DEAR EARTH,

WHY DOES IT
RAIN?

THANKS,
JJ AND BROOKLYN

Earth replied with a smile.

Clouds are made up of tiny water droplets. When they grow they become too heavy. Unable to stay in the sky the water droplets fall to the ground as rain.

Rain gives people, plants, and animals the water they need to live!

Dear Earth,

I love to swim in the ocean, there are so many sea creatures! How can we take care of the ocean for them?

With Love,
Rocean

"Yup its pretty cool down here!" Nathan gives a big thumbs up

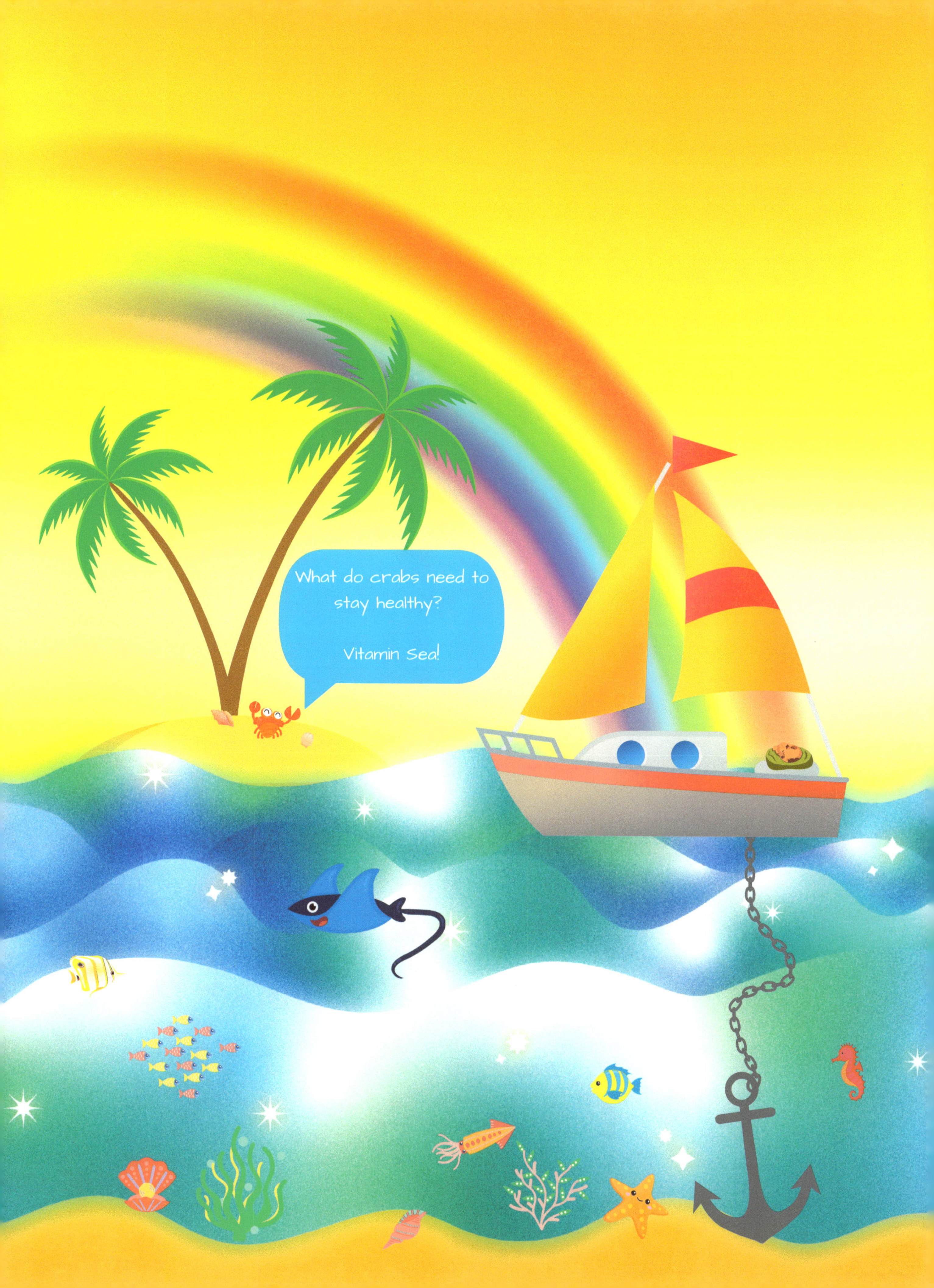
What do crabs need to stay healthy?
Vitamin Sea!

Earth responds with love,

NO!
plastic waste

Lots of plastic ends up in the ocean and its not good for sea creatures.

Here are a few ways you can help!

Carry a reusable water bottle.

Ask for no plastic utensils when ordering takeout.

Reduce. Reuse. Recycle.

Participate in neighborhood and beach clean-ups.

Conserve water by taking shorter showers. Turn off water when brushing your teeth.

When visiting the beach, leave no trash behind. Only footprints.

We depend on the ocean for food and water that supports our climate. THANK YOU for taking care of our oceans!

Dear Earth,

Clouds are so cool!
What are they and
why do they look so different?

Thanks,

Mya and Emmett

Earth says with excitement,

Cirrus clouds are high feathery clouds. They are up so high they are actually made of ice particles.

Cumulus clouds- These clouds look like puffs of cotton!

Stratus clouds look like flat sheets of clouds. These clouds can mean an overcast day or steady rain.

Nimbus clouds- These clouds are dark and seen during a thunderstorm with lightning.

Clouds affect the overall temperature or energy balance of the Earth and play a large role in controlling the planet's long-term climate.

Dear Earth,

What is the
tallest
mountain?

With love,
Luca and Giuliana

Earth replies,

Mount Everest is located in the Himalayan Mountains. Here are some facts about this amazing mountain!

*Mt. Everest is 29,028.87 feet Tall.

*It's peak is on the border between Nepal and China.

Mount Everest is over 60 million years old!

DEAR EARTH,

WHAT IS EARTH DAY AND HOW CAN WE HELP?

WITH LOVE,
VALENTINE, TY, AND JAGER

Mother Earth responds,

Earth Day started April 22, 1970 in the USA. By 1990 people around the world started to celebrate me! Learning more, paying attention to my signs, and finding ways to keep me healthy. I think it's so nice!

Here are a few ways you can celebrate Earth Day!

☀️ Learn about climate change and tell others!

♻️ Reduce, reuse, and recycle!

🛍️ Shop at farmers markets.

🌿 Grow something!

🕊️ Spread the love.

Earth Day

YOU can make a DIFFERENCE!

Dear Earth,

Why is our earth called
the blue planet?

Thanks,
Aspen and Brooke

Earth says,

" I'm 71% water. This is what makes me a cool blue."

Earth is the only known planet with water in our solar system! This is why taking care of our oceans is an important part of keeping our Earth healthy.

Dear Earth,

What is the Aurora Borealis
and where can we find it?

-Thanks!
Delilah, Kansas, and Penelope

This colorful area is located in the cold **ARTIC** and **ANTARCTIC** regions known as the Aurora zone.

The aurora around the North Pole is called the **Aurora Borealis** also known as the **Northern Lights**. An aurora around the South pole is called the **Aurora Australis** or the **Southern Lights**.

The colored light is caused by electrically charged particles from space entering the Earth's upper atmosphere at a very high speed.

Dear Growing Human,

May you always be curious and roam free. You have a big heart and that is a special key. Mountains, weather, and the birds flying high in the sky. Never be shy to ask why?

Each on your own Path doing your Part. I know you will think of me with all of your heart.

As I say good morning and good night to some. Everywhere is magical even where your from!

Just look, and hear the sounds...
Remember, its never goodbye. Its more like see you around!

With lots of love,

Earth

About the author

Olivia Frank is a mother, artist, first-time author and illustrator.
Life for her has always been a creative journey. For years she explored
the Caribbean by sailboat with her husband, one with nature. In 2016
they had a baby boy and took to the road in their motorhome! Inspired
by their travels, she started to write along the way.
Through her books she is inspiring young minds to appreciate
and explore this beautiful earth.

Dear Earth is her first book. With many more books coming soon!
You can visit her website for more info.

ExploreAndWonder.com

She currently resides in Tucson, Arizona with her family.

Do everything
with love.

Never Stop Exploring.

www.ingramcontent.com/pod-product-compliance
Lightning Source LLC
Chambersburg PA
CBHW060857270326
41934CB00003B/180